ALISON

Dante and the Legibility of the Universe: Facts and Narratives

Bernardo Lecture Series, No. 21

Center for Medieval & Renaissance Studies
Binghamton University
State University of New York
Binghamton, NY

© Copyright 2021
Center for Medieval & Renaissance Studies
Binghamton University
State University of New York
Binghamton, NY

Published by
State University of New York Press, Albany

All rights reserved

Printed in the United States of America

No part of this book may be used or reproduced in any manner whatsoever without written permission. No part of this book may be stored in a retrieval system or transmitted in any form or by any means including electronic, electrostatic, magnetic tape, mechanical, photocopying, recording, or otherwise without the prior permission in writing of the publisher.

For information, contact State University of New York Press, Albany, NY
www.sunypress.edu

Library of Congress Cataloging-in-Publication Data

Cornish, Alison
Dante and the Legibility of the Universe: Facts and Narratives / Alison Cornish.
(Bernardo Lecture Series ; No. 21)
ISBN 9781438486949 (pbk. : alk. paper)

Library of Congress Control Number: 2021936505

10 9 8 7 6 5 4 3 2 1

BERNARDO LECTURE SERIES

Editor: Olivia Holmes

Dante and the Legibility of the Universe: Facts and Narratives

In these polarized times, we often accuse others or are accused by others of choosing our facts to suit our narrative of choice. Calling out this prejudicial behavior highlights the superiority of fact over fiction; it is a call to examine facts that "don't fit the narrative." This could be seen as a desire to break out of Plato's cave, out of the "story" told by shadows projected on our screens, to get to the *real* real—not just to the campfire forming the shadows but to the source of all light: the sun, blinding as it might be to anyone accustomed to shadows and darkness. Of course, Plato's Allegory of the Cave is just another narrative, an allegorical one at that, and its fundamental point is that the truth lies somewhere behind or beyond things merely evident to the senses; the truth is ultimately in the realm of the abstract, the mathematical, the irrefutably, axiomatically, and eternally true. Escaping from the cave requires not that we reject the evidence before our eyes but that we read it, and the only way we can read anything—including things that challenge our assumptions and preconceived notions—is to place it in a preexisting narrative. In other words, the only facts we can see are the ones we are looking for.

This inability to see facts has been the subject of several studies and laments. As Elizabeth Kolbert wrote in a 2017 *New Yorker* article, "If reason is designed to generate sound judgments, then it's hard to conceive of a more serious design flaw than confirmation bias."[1] In his blog post "Why Facts Don't Change Our Minds," James Clear recalls that:

> The economist J. K. Galbraith once wrote, "Faced with a choice between changing one's mind and proving there is no need to do so, almost everyone gets busy with the proof."
>
> Leo Tolstoy was even bolder: "The most difficult subjects can be explained to the most slow-witted man if he has not formed any idea of them already; but the simplest

thing cannot be made clear to the most intelligent man if he is firmly persuaded that he knows already, without a shadow of doubt, what is laid before him."²

How, then, might we ever change our minds? If it is not alternate (or alternative) facts that can do it, perhaps an alternative narrative can. Perhaps it is possible to choose among available narratives, especially if one is familiar with narratives, and discover or decide what particular role one is or should be playing. To put it most starkly: Is my life a tragedy or a comedy? Am I a victim or a villain? Am I headed for glory or for shipwreck?

The "moral" of a story generally comes at its end. The *Divine Comedy* is a polyphony of different stories, all of which have come to an end, because this epic is set in the afterlife, from which this life can be finally judged. It is eschatological, which is to say, a vista in retrospect, a view from the end. As you might suspect, this long medieval poem subscribes to a master narrative, an all-encompassing story that—not to put too fine a point on it—has a happy ending. That is why it is called a "comedy." Everything looks different from within that narrative framework. The poem dramatizes that difference—between how things look while you're in the midst of them and how they look beyond the close-up, outside the local frame. What appear to be random facts—a series of unfortunate events—can be discerned as conforming to a larger pattern, structure, or narrative.

Dante's master narrative is both familiar and forgotten. It may not be surprising that it is forgotten to us, since we live in a very different time and place, but it also seems to be forgotten or obscured by characters we meet in his imagined afterlife, judging from the surprise registered by the damned and the saved that things turned out as they did. Dante's narrative is set against other narratives, such as those of the ancient pagans (which is to say non-Christians)—a gesture that enables him to critique his own modernity by measuring it against another, venerable paradigm and delineate what makes modernity different, maybe better, and how it has changed the narrative and shifted the paradigm.

Dante's character, his first-person protagonist, gets lost in the midst of things: "In the middle of our life's journey I found myself in a dark wood [Nel mezzo del cammin di nostra vita / mi ritrovai per una selva oscura]" (*Inferno* 1.1–2).³ He manages to get out of the woods by morning (around line 12 of the 14,233-line poem), reflecting on his survival of a kind of spiritual shipwreck by describing himself as emerging from the deep to the shore ("uscito fuor del pelago a la riva," 1.23). The sun is shining and he looks up; he sees a mountain and aspires to climb it (1.28–60). In metaphoric directional language whose valence is universal, he is now headed up, rather than down, and that is good. It turns out that however much he would like to climb the hill, he finds his way obstructed by impediments allegorically represented as three beasts. His only way around them is to acquire a guide, someone wiser than himself, and try a different route, which, it turns out, is down and not up. Or rather, first down, and then up. Or maybe even what looks like down, but is in fact up. The relevant point for my argument is that the way out is offered by a book—and not the Book that we would expect medieval people to turn to first. Virgil is an ancient pagan author, that is, a non-Christian, and he resides in Hell.

Dante acknowledges him as a book:

> vagliami 'l lungo studio e 'l grande amore
> che m'ha fatto cercar lo tuo volume. (*Inferno* 1.83–84)

This might be translated as something like "may my long and careful reading of your book avail me." Virgil's arrival on the scene to rescue the lost Dante makes it clear that reading that book did come in handy.

In the Middle Ages, reading was understood to be an ethical activity. John Dagenais, writing about the medieval Spanish romance *El libro de buen amor*, put it this way:

> Where we tend to see our texts as webs of language, medieval readers saw a world of human action for good or ill co-extensive with their own. Texts were acts of demonstrative rhetoric that reached out and grabbed the reader, involved him or her in praise and blame, in judgments about effective and ineffective human behavior. . . . They required the reader to take a stand about what he or she read.[4]

In the *Divine Comedy*, the whole house of cards depends, we might say, on the truth of the master narrative. But truth as we experience it is a matter of reading, in fact a matter of choice. This is not the same as saying that we each have "our own truth." As indicated in the first line of Dante's poetic autobiography, where the context is *our* life (*nostra vita*), there is indeed a reality outside individual experience, and it is against this reality that the individual life can be read, can be seen to make sense, to have purpose and direction, or to be way off track.

The book that is Virgil resides in Limbo, the best neighborhood in Hell, among characters and authors of other books. Their placement in Limbo marks them as foreign to Dante's own culture. Limbo is a relatively pleasant place of its residents' own making, their own imagining, and it is clearly not the same as the Christian Heaven, which would be something else entirely and, crucially, something alien to their way of thinking. People in Limbo seem comfortable as well as noble, but a bit sad.

The Christian narrative is certainly present from the beginning of the *Divine Comedy*. As John Freccero pointed out so richly, the strange allegorical landscape of the first canto of the poem is a "region of unlikeness"—a phrase that originated perhaps in Plato's *Statesman* (as Margaret Ferguson has found), where the stranger describes a universe gone off the rails as "in the bottomless abyss of unlikeness," but became equated in Judeo-Christian thought with Exodus and exile, with wandering in the desert.[5] To be in the region of unlikeness might be understood as a failure to perceive likeness or resemblance; a failure to recognize that there is a narrative, rather than just random suffering; and that what is happening to you now is like a story that is already written: a story of exodus, which is a tale not of being lost but of patiently making one's way out of the desert into the promised land; or, to summarize a parallel narrative, the one told in Virgil's *Aeneid*, the journey out of an exploded city, the city of Troy, to found the seat of Empire, the city of Rome.

Stories informed by prior stories became what poststructuralist literary critic Julia Kristeva called "intertextuality": "other texts in a text."[6] My point here is that this is not just the way literature works; it is the way life works. We can see this in popular and even clinical psychology. Dan McAdams and Erika Manczak write about how people perform "autobiographical reasoning," characterized by "identifying lessons learned or insights gained in life experiences, marking development or growth through sequences of scenes, and showing how specific life episodes illustrate enduring truths about the self."[7] In her article "Life's Stories," citing this industry standard, Julie Beck comments: "Once certain stories get embedded into the culture, they become master narratives—blueprints for people to follow when structuring their own stories, for better or worse. One such blueprint is your standard 'go to school, graduate, get a job, get married, have kids.'"[8] She goes on to characterize a "master narrative" or "blueprint" as both "helpful script" and "pernicious frame"; she asserts, "these scripts evolve as culture evolves." It is interesting that even though she dismisses medieval sorts of narratives, such as "being possessed by demons," as the sort of thing that would be "out of place" today, she observes that one of the main narratives is a "redemption story." The other sort of story she describes is the "contamination sequence," as in, "The cruise was amazing until we all got food poisoning." According to experts, the contamination theme is a sign of "poorer mental health." Yet if a redemption story is, even in a purely secular article and a purely secular discipline, a sign of good mental health, it is clearly something that goes pretty deep and is not a product of cultural evolution.

What I am arguing, as a literary scholar and reader of Dante, is that there is a need not just for stories but for books (or whatever currently serves the function that books once did) as containers and transmitters of culture—despite the obvious obsolescence of the medium—and particularly for old books, whether or not they are immediately identifiable as products of our "own" specific culture. It is not so much prescriptive as descriptive to recognize that we are always and everywhere called to read, since the universe is basically a book, written in the language of mathematics, Galileo says, or bound by love into a single volume, as Dante says at the very end of his own book. The ability to read what is set before us entails freedom and high stakes, as misreadings can be costly—or sometimes beneficial. The *Divine Comedy* is like other books that you can read however you want to, but it does have a preferred narrative, which is to say, a narrative the author thinks is true or chooses to believe, and his story dramatizes the risks and rewards of different ways of reading, or what we might call competing narratives.

The locus classicus for the scene of reading in the *Divine Comedy* is the episode of Paolo and Francesca among the Lustful in the fifth canto of the *Inferno*. It is surely influenced by other famous episodes of reading—Augustine's conversion in the garden when he hears children calling "Take up and read," or Abelard's account of seducing Heloise during their tutorials over a book. As Elena Lombardi observes, the canto of Francesca is "the canto with the greatest number of references to the act of reading."⁹ Francesca's first account of her tragic tale is in three succinct acts, in which Love did three things: Love, which is kindled quickly in the gentle heart, seized her companion by means of her beautiful body; Love, which absolves no one from reciprocating love, seized her by means of his attractive appearance; and Love led them to one death.

> Amor, ch'al cor gentil ratto s'apprende,
> prese costui de la bella persona
> che mi fu tolta; e 'l modo ancor m'offende.
> Amor, ch'a nullo amato amar perdona,
> mi prese del costui piacer sì forte,
> che, come vedi, ancor non m'abbandona.
> Amor condusse noi ad una morte. (*Inferno* 5.100–106)

> [Love, that is quickly kindled in the gentle heart seized him by means of the beautiful body that was taken from me (and it still offends me how). Love, that pardons no one loved from loving in return, seized me by means of his attractiveness so strongly that, as you see, it still does not leave me. Love led us to a single death.]

But it is Dante's probing question, his desire to know the details, the sort of prurience inspired by romance (as well as pornography), that induces her to narrate the scene of their reading. Overcome with emotion, Dante asks by what means and how in the time of the sweet sighs they came to recognize their fearful (or doubtful) desires (*Inferno* 5.118–20).

So Francesca narrates that they were reading out of a big book, a very big book, spanning many volumes. It was written in a language she understood. Most of the books in the world around her were in a bookish language that would require a certain kind of education that she wasn't given, because it would not have been necessary to her social station. But this book was written in a spoken tongue with which she was familiar. It was not exactly the one she used to speak to her servants, her children, and her husband or the slightly different one she heard as a child, from her parents, her nurse, and the other children in the courtyard, but it was close enough that she could follow the plot and imagine what the book describes. It describes another world, another place, long ago, with people in it who are both like and unlike the people she knows. The ladies are beautiful and the men are gallant, and the best ones are in love. She was not alone in reading—rather, she was alone with another person—perhaps because she did not know how to read, perhaps because she preferred to listen to another person read, or perhaps because it is more enjoyable to read in the company of another. The book narrates extraordinary adventures and forbidden longings—of the sort that made her blush, particularly because she was not alone but in the company of a young man who was very handsome and not her husband. They were both enjoying the book, especially those parts that made their eyes meet and their cheeks flush. They kept reading until one of those moments overcame them. The book told of Lancelot and how love gripped him. But it was only when they read how the desired smile was kissed by so great a lover that the woman's reading partner kissed her mouth all trembling, and that day they read no further.

> Quando leggemmo il disïato riso
> esser basciato da cotanto amante,
> questi, che mai da me non fia diviso,
> la bocca mi basciò tutto tremante.
> Galeotto fu 'l libro e chi lo scrisse:
> quel giorno più non vi leggemmo avante. (*Inferno* 5.133–38)

[When we read that the desired smile was kissed by so great a lover, this one, who never shall be parted from me, kissed my mouth all trembling. Gallehault was the book and he who wrote it. That day we read no further.]

In a nutshell, this is the famous story of Dante's Francesca, damned—damned!—for love. As many readers have pointed out, reading the effect of the book on Francesca has a similar effect on Dante, who hears her story and faints dead away, and then on us, who in turn read of his experience of her experience and have our own experience. This *punto*, this point in the book where the lovers are impelled to abandon the book and embrace each other like the characters in it, is a universally exhilarating and terrifying moment because it is exhilarating to discover that you love and that what or whom you love, loves you back, and terrifying that this might entail the destruction or abandonment of everything else you hold dear. For this, evidently, she is thrown into Hell. Who put her there? Was it Dante, who only feigned sympathy? Or was it the God of whose grim judgments Dante is only the dutiful reporter? In the preface to his 1816 poem *Story of Rimini*, English Romantic poet and essayist Leigh Hunt puts the blame squarely on the joyless and somewhat vindictive medieval poet: "We even lose sight of the place, in which the saturnine poet, according to his summary way of disposing both of friends and enemies, has thought proper to put the sufferers; and see the whole melancholy absurdity of his theology, in spite of itself, falling to nothing before one genuine impulse of the affections."[10]

But on our theme of reading: on its most superficial level, it seems to be a story about the dangers of romantic literature, especially for women, perhaps especially in a repressive society brutally intolerant of women's pleasure and autonomy. Indeed, without that element of the forbidden or transgressive, would the discovery be anywhere nearly so exhilarating? Although she herself calls that moment of recognition (when they recognized their fearful desires) a defeat ("that moment vanquished us [ma solo un punto fu quel che ci vinse]"), it can and has been read as a victory. When she says of the unnamed weeping spirit accompanying her on the hellish storm, "he, who never shall be parted from me, kissed my mouth all trembling," it appears to be a triumph of love over death, a love that makes the lovers forever inseparable, despite the constraints of religion, family, and society, in the face of all objections and judgments, even the judgment of Hell itself.

> Quando leggemmo il disïato riso
> esser basciato da cotanto amante,
> questi, che mai da me non fia diviso,
> la bocca mi basciò tutto tremante. (*Inferno* 5.133–36)

> [When we read that the desired smile was kissed by so great a lover, this one, who never shall be parted from me, kissed my mouth all trembling.]

A book made this happen, opened new worlds to her, let her see inside her own heart and recognize her love. It is a revelation, and it is mediated. In the end (is it a curse? or just a matter of fact?) she calls the book and its author a name, a name she has learned from the book: *Galeotto* ("Galeotto fu 'l libro e chi lo scrisse: / quel giorno più non vi leggemmo avante [Gallehault was the book and he who wrote it. That day we read no farther in it]," *Inferno* 5.137–38). The book was a Gallehault, and so was its author. You would have to have read the book or have been told about it by someone else to know that in the romance she was reading, Gallehault was the go-between, the liaison who brought Lancelot, loyal knight of King Arthur, together with Guinevere, Arthur's wife, into the forbidden, passionate, and adulterous affair that (as the book recounts much later) eventually brings down Camelot. What she means, then, is that the book was a go-between, an intermediary, a panderer, an agent of seduction. It bears the blame, or the credit, for her own story.

    Are some books, therefore, guilty? Should they be banned? Does it depend on whether their potentially transformative effect is considered for good or ill? If the book gave Francesca her one taste of self-determination, pleasure, or what we sometimes call "true love," it might be seen as a very good book indeed, a welcome gift to oppressed women, which seems to be why Boccaccio gave the subtitle of "Gallehault" to his long book with salacious tales for the consolation of ladies. If, however, as Francesca seems to suggest, the book can lead people, perhaps especially women, perhaps especially women as sheltered and naive as herself, to their ruin, perhaps it should be banned or at least excoriated in such a way as to dissuade anyone from reading it or taking it seriously. Recently scholars have pointed out a letter that Boccaccio wrote to a friend in Florence, warning him not to let his daughters read the *Decameron*, quite in contradiction to the book's stated claim that the author wrote it for the ladies.[11]

    Francesca's story dramatizes the act of reading and its potentially disastrous consequences. As scholars have long pointed out, Francesca obviously misreads the very passage that she claims so affected her: in the medieval French romance that she is reading, the so-called *Prose Lancelot*, Guinevere, with a great deal of help and encouragement from Gallehault, takes the initiative to kiss Lancelot who, however great a knight, was indeed shaking like a leaf.[12] A particularly revealing illustration can be found in a French manuscript almost exactly contemporary with Dante's writing of this canto, preserved in the Morgan Library, where Gallehault presides over the scene at the apex of a triangle, his left arm pushing Guinevere toward Lancelot, who looks somewhat alarmed and rests his elbow on Gallehault's lap. Another, in the so-called Rochefoucauld Grail illuminated manuscript, of similar date and provenance, depicts Lancelot almost recoiling as an advancing Gallehault grips his right wrist and Guinevere with her left hand lifts his chin toward her mouth,[13]

The fact that Francesca misremembers, misreads, or misrepresents who kissed whom calls into question her own witness, particularly with regard to agency, or, to put it in more morally determined terms: fault. In her first spectacularly concise narrative of the events, she ascribes all agency to Amor, an irresistible power or deity who quickly takes hold particularly of noble, gentle, or soft hearts by means of beautiful people, a god who demands that love be reciprocated and who led the lovers to their common death.

We could also say Francesca did not simply read a book, she let the book read her. By this I mean that the book told her what part she might be playing in her own drama—the part of Guinevere in the presence of her Lancelot in a world ruled by the god of Love. Yet a way she might have read the book differently is suggested by many of the things she says. She would like to be kinder and more useful to the visitor to Hell, whom she addresses as "nice animal [O animal grazïoso e benigno]," than she can be. She would generously pray for his peace, she says, "if the king of the universe were my friend" ("se fosse amico il re de l'universo, / noi pregheremmo lui de la tua pace [if the king of the universe were a friend of ours, we would pray to him for your peace]," *Inferno* 5.91–92). In romances, the term *friend, amico* (or in the French, *ami*) meant "lover." But evidently, because she uses the past subjunctive contrary to fact, she is not so fortunate to have intimate friends in such high places. It exudes a certain regret, perhaps regret in her choice of lover. At the crucial moment, when Francesca and her brother-in-law read how "the desired smile was kissed by so great a lover," it would seem that the greatest of lovers must be Lancelot. In brutal contrast, at that very moment, to have your mouth kissed by the sweaty-palmed fellow sitting next to you in the room, the unnamed "this one" from whom you will now never be parted, might be something of a disappointment, if not total Hell. But if the king of the universe could be a friend, indeed, a lover, an *ami*, would *He* not be the greatest lover of all?

When Francesca states axiomatically that "Love pardons no beloved from loving in return [Amor, ch'a nullo amato amar perdona]," as if to say that all invitations must be accepted, one might ponder the first and foundational invitation to love. As a chivalrous Italian puts it later in the poem, the simple little soul issues from the hand of Him who loves her, who desires her, who courts her, and makes love to her. These are all possible translations of the verb *vagheggia*:

> Esce di mano a lui che la vagheggia
> prima che sia, a guisa di fanciulla
> che piangendo e ridendo pargoleggia,
> l'anima semplicetta che sa nulla,
> salvo che, mossa da lieto fattore,
> volontier torna a ciò che la trastulla. (*Purgatorio* 16.85–90)

> [The simple, little soul issues from the hand of him who desires her before she even is. Like a little girl who plays, weeping and laughing, who knows nothing except, moved by a happy Maker, she willingly turns to whatever delights her.]

The simple soul, grammatically feminine, is like a little girl, playing, weeping, and laughing. In her radical innocence, knowing nothing, she turns to whatever delights her, precisely because she is moved in the first place by happiness, the happiness that made her. That is love's invitation: to reciprocate. The phrase that Francesca uses to excuse her capitulation to her brother-in-law's desires—"love pardons no one who is loved from loving in return"—is actually an indictment of her own failure to reciprocate the love that really was offered first.

Many readers have pointed out that Francesca's mistake was not necessarily to read the book she was reading, which was a romance, but to stop reading it in the middle—in the middle of a sentence, in fact, as Lombardi notes—and not follow it through to the end, since the *Prose Lancelot* actually contains a lesson about the rippling negative repercussions wrought by a single love affair. I am arguing that in her account of what happened, of who did what to whom first (Love caused Paolo to love her first, a love she was bound to return), she also skips over the beginning of the story. Francesca skips over the fact that there was a first lover, who loved her first, a lover even greater than Lancelot. For readers who have reached the end of the poem, there is nothing prior to love. Love is what motivates the whole universe, what "moves the sun and the other stars [l'amor che move il sole e l'altre stelle]" (*Paradiso* 33.135). Love is also what binds up, binds together, all the scattered accidents, all the apparently random occurrences, the inclinations, the mistakes, the false starts, into a single volume, a single book ("legato con amore in un volume," *Paradiso* 33.86).

If "all you need is love," or "it doesn't matter who you love or how you love, but *that* you love" (as the Beatles and Rod McKuen advise us), then what is love doing in Hell?[14] And not only in the Circle of the Lustful. Particularly jarring to our modern sentiments is the claim that love—in fact, the "first love," which is essentially God, or more specifically, the Holy Spirit—actually made Hell. Inscribed on the Gates of Hell, like Marcus Agrippa on the front of the Pantheon, is the signature of the architect. The gate reads: "fecemi la divina podestate, / la somma sapïenza e 'l primo amore [I was made by the divine power, the highest wisdom, and the first love]" (*Inferno* 3.5–6). Now if the "first love" made Hell, we might want to look around for alternatives. Yet the love of Francesca's narrative, the one that demanded she reciprocate, the one that led her to death and damnation seems to have been equally fatal. Does love inexorably lead to death? Or to Hell? Or is love simply the motivator whichever way one is headed and therefore neutral?

A facile modern reading of Francesca's predicament is to lament her misfortune of being born in a dark time when her love (indeed, any "true" love), freely chosen, was forbidden by others and society. It was illegitimate, outside the law, outside cultural norms that were established perhaps only by men (the patriarchy) and oppressively imposed on women against their will. This explains the "triumphal" reading. Francesca breaks through such arbitrary and unjust strictures; she has agency, she touches joy. She claims to have been happy—a happiness that was too short-lived and unjustly cut short. "No greater sorrow is there," she says, "than to recall happiness in misery [Nessun maggior dolore / che ricordarsi del tempo felice / ne la miseria]" (5.121–23). Who are we to question whether she was "really" happy in adultery? Especially when we suspect (and Boccaccio spun out the plausible details) that she was unhappy in her marriage. Who is to say whether some loves are good and others bad?

Olivia Holmes reminds us that there is a long tradition of portraying moral choice as erotic choice, usually from the male perspective, between "two women, one dark and one light," one a virgin, one a whore.[15] As Holmes traces throughout Dante's works and inherited culture, the alternatives might be between wisdom and folly, earthly and divine, sensual and spiritual, Lady Philosophy or the sirens. These adjectives and epithets prompt the question: what makes something dark or light, virgin or whore? Let us interrogate Francesca about why her choice might have been the wrong one. The most compelling argument against her freely chosen love is the fact that she herself says she is not happy; in fact, she is miserable, despite being conjoined forever with her supposed beloved. Again, in the "triumphal" reading, "forever" is defiant; it indicates a love that survives even death. Alternatively, "forever" is a long time to spend alongside someone who does not make you happy. And Paolo—surely this pains him (he never seems to stop crying)—is clearly not making her happy. That is because they are being punished, you say, because someone stuck them in Hell. There is no earthly love that can make people happy if the external conditions are brutal enough. That is precisely the point, Dante might say.

There is also embedded in her account what it was that she, they, actually loved. As I have already suggested, it seems pretty clear that Francesca fell in love not with Paolo but with Lancelot, the image of "so great a lover." Moreover, in her very brief account of Love's deeds, she indicates that she and her lover were "taken," "seized," or "gripped" by the corporeal beauty of the other. He by her *persona*, or body, or physical appearance; she by his *piacere*, his attractiveness, what the old troubadour poets called *plazer*.

There is absolutely nothing wrong with being smitten by a beautiful body. Dante says as much, under interrogation about love in Heaven (as authoritative a circumstance as the poem might offer), when he says that Beatrice originally entered through his eyes "with the fire that makes him still burn [col foco ond' io sempr' ardo]" (*Paradiso* 26.15). Beatrice herself, with astonishing immodesty, describes her physical body—her limbs that are now scattered in the Earth—as the most beautiful thing that Dante ever encountered, either in real life, or in artistic representation.

> Mai non t'appresentò natura o arte
> piacer, quanto le belle membra in ch'io
> rinchiusa fui, e che so' 'n terra sparte
> e se 'l sommo piacer sì ti fallio . . . (*Purgatorio* 31.49–52)

[Never did nature or art put before you such beauty as had the beautiful limbs in which I was enclosed, and that are scattered in the earth; and if the highest pleasure/beauty/physical attractiveness thus failed you . . .]

Hers was a body that (at least while she lived and he could see it) was leading him on a virtuous path. That's what she claims: "for a while I sustained him with my face [alcun tempo ll sostenni col mio volto]," "leading him with me in the right direction [meco il menava in dritta parte vòlto]"; "he loved me less when I was no longer flesh and became spirit, in which my beauty and power increased [Quando di carne a spirto era salita, / e bellezza e virtù cresciuta m'era, / fu' io a lui men cara e men gradita]"; and instead he followed "false images of good [imagini di ben seguendo false]." Indeed, the definition of "false image" is one that does not keep its promises ("che nulla promession rendono intera," *Purgatorio* 30.121–32).

The issue is not that beauty is skin deep or that we should love the "person" rather than what Francesca means by *persona* (body). It is pretty clear that the only things we can love are, precisely, images. The well-informed Virgil will explain that the soul abstracts images from reality and opens them up internally, and if it bends toward that unfolded image, that bending is love:

> Vostra apprensiva da esser verace
> tragge intenzione, e dentro a voi la spiega,
> sì che l'animo ad essa volger face;
> e se, rivolto, inver' di lei si piega,
> quel piegare è amor, quell' è natura
> che per piacer di novo in voi si lega. (*Purgatorio* 18.22–27)

> [Your faculty of apprehension draws an intention from a real thing, and unfolds it within you, so that it makes the mind turn toward it; and if, thus turned, the mind bends toward it, that bending is love: that is the nature that is bound in you again by pleasure.]

So the problem is that we always and only fall in love with images—in fact, images of our own making. The judgment of whether an image is false or true, good or bad, comes with whether it can deliver on its promise that it can make us happy. Virgil makes this distinction in a lecture on love in the previous canto. What we learn there is that everything that *is* is to some extent good; everything that *is* loves, and loves what it perceives as at least a glimmer of the good. So much for McKuen's pseudo-profound sentiment: "it's only important *that* you love," not what or how, since neither Creator nor creature (which covers everybody and everything) ever existed that did not have love:

> "Né creator né creatura mai,"
> cominciò el, "figliuol, fu sanza amore,
> o naturale o d'animo; e tu 'l sai." (*Purgatorio* 17.91–93)

> ["Neither creator nor creature was ever without love, son," he began, "either natural or mental; and this you know."]

The problem, as Virgil logically lays out, is that you can have too much or too little love for good things, or you can love the wrong thing. The only wrong object of love is not the wrong person, or the wrong good, but wanting something that is not good for someone else: "when people desire evil for their neighbor [che 'l mal che s'ama è del prossimo]" (*Purgatorio* 17.113), that is, when they're "haters," as some might say today. This wrong love, or desire for evil, underlies the first three capital sins: pride, envy, and wrath. Lust, Francesca's sin, is not a wrong love; it is in the category of excess. There are many goods that we apprehend confusedly, in which we think our minds may rest, and that is what we desire, but some goods, although good, are not what make people happy.[16] Lust, like gluttony and greed, is to abandon oneself excessively or entirely to such things that will, in the end, disappoint. To say that this is God's judgment is another way of saying it is the truth of the matter. The romance that pretends otherwise is a lie.

It is not hard to understand why Francesca's story is gripping. It does to us what the story of Lancelot and Guinevere did to her. It seizes our sympathies. It makes us identify with her. It is perhaps *the* story: how we come to love what we love and how we become aware of it. Her scene of reading answers Dante's question of how it happened. It is a question demanding a story. More fundamentally, it is a question about how: by what means and by what medium? Her answer involves what we would call media: a handheld device that can increase knowledge and kindle desire. It is not simply that she should "get off her phone" and pay attention to the reality around her. It is precisely the move from reading to reality that got her in trouble (some people say the lovers read too little; others say they read too much). The disaster happens by failing to see the one story contained in the frame of another, not just in the context of the *Prose Lancelot* but in a larger romance altogether. I have already observed that the very dictate Francesca professes, that Love absolves no one loved from loving in return, would have required her to reciprocate the first love, who "woos her [che la vagheggia]" even before she existed. In her courtly imagination, in the narrative she believes, God is a king who dispenses favors to his friends and lovers. Even in that paradigm, it would behoove her to stay loyal, keep her promises, or simply fulfill her duty, in fact, to the king himself and not betray him by transferring her love to one of his vassals.

When we talk about the episode as giving the reader a warning against sensual love, it falls on deaf ears—not just our own, because we no longer believe in medieval cultural norms where "medieval" is a value judgment (and not a positive one!) and not just a chronological descriptor—but also on those of "love's faithful," as Dante called them when he joined the company of Tuscan love poets who wrote in an ideology of refined, courtly love in which the enamored heart was by definition noble and the lady, more exalted still, became a kind of angel. Francesca speaks that language ("love that is kindled quickly in the gentle heart [amor ch'al cor gentil ratto s'apprende]") and subscribes to that ideology, as do we: love ennobles. The point of her damnation, excogitated by the self-reflective poet and not by some unmerciful God, might be to expose the distance between romance and reality, between the desired smile and the trembling mouth, between what we promise and what we do, between narrative and fact. But, I submit, what is depicted in *Inferno* 5 is not a failure of imaginative literature but a failure not to imagine enough, to reduce the story down to the literal, corporeal *mouth* and not follow it upward into the metaphorical "desired smile"—what Dante refers to later in the *Paradiso* as the "smile of the universe [riso dell'universo]" (*Paradiso* 27.4–5).

My purpose is not to damn Francesca to Hell; my sympathies are entirely with her. She too has become a book, a romantic story, with which it is quite possible to identify. My purpose is to argue that we are always reading books or subscribing to certain narratives—some sustained by popular culture, some latent in our cultural inheritance. Some narratives are persistent, so that Dante can see the founding of

Troy as consonant with the story of Exodus and even the story of salvation, stories Virgil neither knew nor imagined. We never have just the facts, and our story is never solely our own. Elizabeth Kolbert invokes the observations of Steven Sloman and Philip Fernbach about why "we never think alone": "We've been relying on one another's expertise ever since we figured out how to hunt together, which was probably a key development in our evolutionary history." This "fundamentally communal nature" of what it is we think we know is what explains "why we often assume we know more than we really do" and "why political opinions and false beliefs are so hard to change."[17] Patricia Crone puts this another way. She observes that unlike other animals, "hominids are forced to supplement their deficient genetic programming with culture." In explaining the universal human phenomena of religions, philosophies, moralities, or ideologies, she writes:

> No human society on earth, however primitive, has managed without additional principles. The point about these principles is that because they are not given by nature, they have to be invented; society has to be based on something made up. The invented element may take the form of deities or abstract concepts such as progress or proletarian struggle; but whatever they are, we are here confronted with an irreducible oddity about all human societies: all are strung around figments of the human imagination.[18]

It is never a question of thinking or even reading "alone" (Francesca says that she and Paolo were "alone and unsuspecting").[19] There is always a narrative in play and we can never get "just the facts." We are always looking for the moral of the story and wanting to know how it ends. The purpose of reading, and rereading, which must be pleasurable if we're going to do it (Dante says it was love that made him search Virgil's volume) is to get at the truth: where romance coincides with reality.

Notes

1. Elizabeth Kolbert, "That's What You Think: Why Reason and Evidence Won't Change Our Minds," *New Yorker*, February 19, 2017, 66–71, 70.

2. James Clear, "Why Facts Don't Change Minds," *James Clear* (blog), https://jamesclear.com/why-facts-dont-change-minds (accessed March 9, 2021). J. K. Galbraith, "How Keynes Came to America," in *A Contemporary Guide to Economics, Peace, and Laughter*, ed. Andrea D. Williams (Boston: Houghton Mifflin, 1971), 50. Leo Tolstoy, *The Kingdom of God Is Within You*, trans. Constance Garnett (New York: Cassell, 1894), 49.

3. Citations of the *Divine Comedy* are from *La Commedia secondo l'antica vulgata*, ed. Giorgio Petrocchi (Turin: Einaudi, 1975). Translations are mine.

4. John Dagenais, *The Ethics of Reading in Manuscript Culture: Glossing the Libro de buen amor* (Princeton, NJ: Princeton University Press, 1994), xvii.

5. John Freccero, "Dante's Prologue Scene," *Dante Studies* 84 (1966): 1–25. Margaret Ferguson, "Saint Augustine's Region of Unlikeness: The Crossing of Exile and Language," in *Innovations of Antiquity*, ed. Daniel Selden and Ralph Hexter (New York: Routledge, 1992), 69–94.

6. Kristeva's views as summarized by María Jesús Martínez Alfaro, "Intertextuality: Origins and Development of the Concept," *Atlantis* 18 (1996): 268.

7. Dan McAdams and Erika Manczak, "Personality and the Life Story," in *APA Handbook of Personality and Social Psychology*, ed. D. P. McAdams and E. Manczak (Washington, DC: American Psychological Association Press, 2015), 4:425–46.

8. Julie Beck, "Life's Stories," *Atlantic*, August 10, 2015, https://www.theatlantic.com/health/archive/2015/08/life-stories-narrative-psychology-redemption-mental-health/400796/.

9. Elena Lombardi, "Reading," in *The Wings of the Dove* (Montreal: McGill-Queen's University Press, 2012), 212–47.

10. Leigh Hunt, *The Selected Writings of Leigh Hunt*, ed. Robert Morrison and Michael Eberle-Sinatra (London: Pickering and Chatto, 2003), 5:165. Pointed out by Martin Eisner in "The Word Made Flesh in *Inferno* 5: Francesca Reading and the Figure of the Annunciation," *Dante Studies*

131 (2013): 51–72. See also Michael Steier, *Byron, Hunt, and the Politics of Literary Engagement* (New York: Routledge, 2019).

11. Renzo Bragantini, "L'amicizia, la fama, il libro: sulla seconda epistola a Mainardo Cavalcanti," in *Boccaccio 1313–2013*, ed. Francesco Ciabattoni, Elsa Filosa, and Kristina Olson (Ravenna: Longo, 2015), 107–15.

12. Anna Hatcher and Mark Musa, "The Kiss: *Inferno* V and the Old French Prose *Lancelot*," *Comparative Literature* 20 (1968): 97–109. Susan Noakes, "The Double Misreading of Paolo and Francesca," in *Dante*, ed. Harold Bloom (New York: Chelsea House, 1986), 151–66.

13. Morgan Library MS M.0805, Northwestern France, ca. 1310–1315, fol. 67r, http://ica.themorgan.org/manuscript/page/49/147055. Amsterdam, Biblioteca Philosophica Hermetica MS 1, ii, f. 140, http://www.pitt.edu/~medart/homepage/arthur.html.

14. William Murray, "Says Rod McKuen: 'It Doesn't Matter Who You Love or How You Love, But That You Love!,'" *New York Times*, April 4, 1971, 32–33, col. 3.

15. Olivia Holmes, *Dante's Two Beloveds: Ethics and Erotics in the Divine Comedy* (New Haven, CT: Yale University Press, 2008), 2.

16. "Ciascun confusamente un bene apprende / nel qual si queti l'animo, e disira . . . Altro ben è che non fa l'uom felice; / non è felicità" (*Purgatorio* 17.127–34).

17. Steven Sloman and Philip Fernbach, *The Knowledge Illusion: Why We Never Think Alone* (New York: Riverhead, 2017), cited in Kolbert, "That's What You Think."

18. Patricia Crone, *Pre Industrial Societies: Anatomy of the Pre-Modern World* (Oxford: Blackwell, 1989), 144–45.

19. Laura Miles, "The Origins and Development of the Virgin Mary's Book at the Annunciation," *Speculum* 89.3 (2014): 632–69, observes that the iconography of the book is connected with Mary's solitude, and her solitude is connected with her virginity, which is essential to the miracle. In the last chapter of her book on reading, *Una meravigliosa solitudine:*

l'arte di leggere nell'Europa moderna (Turin: Einaudi, 2019), Lina Bolzoni recalls Proust's objection to Ruskin's idealizing notion of reading as a "conversation," insisting instead on the necessity of solitude.

Alison Cornish is Professor of Italian at New York University and President of the Dante Society of America. She has published two monographs, *Reading Dante's Stars* (Yale, 2000) and *Vernacular Translation in Dante's Italy: Illiterate Literature* (Cambridge 2011), a commentary on Stanley Lombardo's translation of Dante's *Paradiso* (Hackett, 2017), and a number of articles on the three crowns of Italian literature. In this centenary year (2021) she has organized a year-long podcasting project: *Canto per Canto: Conversations with Dante in Our Time.*

The Aldo S. Bernardo Fund

The Aldo S. Bernardo Fund is the endowment fund for the Center for Medieval and Renaissance Studies at Binghamton University (State University of New York). Established in 1989 by a gift from the founding co-director of the Center, the fund aims to support Center programs with a special emphasis on medieval and Renaissance Italian studies. Since its inception, the Bernardo Fund has supported the Bernardo Lecture series as well as book purchases for the Bartle Library. The endowment has continued to develop and is now also used to support a range of programs associated with the Center's teaching and research activities.

The Research Foundation of Binghamton University, which is a private, not-for-profit corporation chartered under the laws of the State of New York, receives tax deductible donations on behalf of the Bernardo Fund.

The Aldo S. Bernardo Lecture Series in the Humanities honors the late Professor Aldo S. Bernardo, his scholarship in medieval Italian literature, and his service to Binghamton University as Professor of Romance Languages and University Distinguished Service Professor. The Bernardo Lecture Series is endowed by the Bernardo Fund and administered by the Center for Medieval and Renaissance Studies (CEMERS), which Professor Bernardo co-founded and co-directed with Professor Bernard Huppé from 1966 to 1973. The series offers annual lectures by distinguished scholars on topics related to Professor Bernardo's primary fields of interest—medieval and Renaissance Italian literature, with a particular focus on Dante Studies, and intellectual history.

The Occasional Papers: Earlier Volumes

1. Robert Hollander, *Dante and Paul's "Five Words with Understanding"* (1990). Five words spoken with understanding are preferable to "ten thousand words in an unknown tongue." With insight and wit, Hollander analyzes speeches of Nimrod (*Inferno* 31) and Plutus (*Inferno* 7) and other instances of garbled or mixed speech.

2. Joan M. Ferrante, *Dante's Beatrice: Priest of an Androgynous God* (1991). Beatrice leads Dante to see a feminine side in God, humanity, and himself. In *Paradise,* he learns to speak of the souls of men as female and the souls of women as male, and to see God as androgynous. Ferrante examines Beatrice's roles of priest, confessor, and teacher of theology, and as a Christ figure.

3. Ciriaco Morón Arroyo, *Celestina and Castilian Humanism at the End of the Fifteenth Century* (1992). Arroyo addresses major questions that have challenged and divided Celestina scholars: the Jewish ancestry of its main author; the relationship of the overt moral intention to artistic character, and the location of the work at the cultural crossroads between medieval and humanistic ways of thinking and writing.

4. Thomas M. Greene, *Besieging the Castle of Ladies* (1993). Greene traces the mysterious motif of the castle defended by women across centuries, regions, and cultural expressions—e.g., an early chronicle, a staged game, the *Roman de la Rose,* English manuscript illuminations, French ivory caskets, and early modern versions. Each instance, like the entire series, poses questions about sexual politics and sexual control.

5. Peter K. Marshall, *Servius and Commentary of Virgil* (1994). Marshall traces the importance and influence, in the wake of Tiberius Claudius Donatus, of Servius's Commentaries in the Middle Ages and Renaissance, especially on the *magistri,* the *grammatici,* and the mythographers.

6. John Freccero, *Dante's Cosmos* (1995). In this intricate but highly readable account of Dante's cosmology, Freccero notes that the

Paradiso may be considered a medieval version of science fiction. However, whereas modern writers of science fiction tend to select a theme that will best illustrate a particular scientific theory, Freccero argues that "Dante chooses his science to fit his theme."

7. Sara Sturm-Maddox, *Dante and Petrarch: The Earthly Paradise Revisited* (1996). The nature and significance of Petrarch's indebtedness to Dante in the *Rime Sparse,* Sturm-Maddox argues, is revealed not only in the many individual poems or isolated echoes disclosed by recent studies. Here it is explored in a strategically placed sequence of poems, the well known *canzoni* 125–127. In each of them Sturm-Maddox finds the reinscription of elements drawn from the scene of Dante's encounter with Beatrice in the Earthly Paradise.

8. William J. Kennedy, *Totems for Defense and Illustration of Taboo: Sites of Petrarchism in Renaissance Europe* (1998). Critical commentaries appended to early printed editions of Petrarch's *Rime Sparse,* Kennedy argues, inflected the reception and understanding of Petrarch's vernacular poetry in Renaissance Europe. As a consequence, the author's expression of his specific Italian social, cultural, and political identity came to acquire a protonationalist value for his later readers. The Petrarchan sonnet, the most widespread vernacular literary mode in sixteenth-century Europe, became a site for early expressions of national sentiment. Kennedy explores this phenomenon in the poetry of Du Bellay in France and of Philip Sidney and his niece Mary Worth in England.

9. Teodolinda Barolini, *Desire and Death, or Francesca and Guido Cavalcanti: Inferno 5 in its Lyric Context* (1997). Barolini explores the lyric context of *Inferno* 5, paying particular attention to how Italian lyric poets such as Giacomo da Lentini, Guido delle Colonne, Guittone d'Arezzo, Guido Cavalcanti, and Dante himself had framed the issue of desire insufficiently controlled by reason. Pointing to Cavalcanti's "che la 'ntenzione per ragione vale" (from "Donna me prega") as the intertext of Dante's "che la ragion sommettono al talento" (*Inferno* 5.39), Barolini reads *Inferno* 5 as a response to Cavalcanti. Moreover, by looking at the views of love evidenced in Dante's own lyrics (e.g., "Lo doloroso amor," the "rime petrose,"

"Io sono stato con Amore insieme," "Amor, da che convien pur ch' io mi doglia," and "Doglia mi reca ne lo core ardire"), the essay reconstructs the complex and arduous ideological pathway that Dante traversed to reach *Inferno 5.*

10. Maria Rosa Menocal, *Writing Without Footnotes: The Role of the Medievalist in Contemporary Intellectual Life* (1999). Menocal argues that intellectual engagement with a public beyond the walls of our own specialties, and even beyond the walls of the academy, was long a commonplace and significant part of our work as professors and writers in the humanities. In reconceptualizing our place in the academy, a task called for by the variety of crises that threaten to make of literary studies a small and insular corner of that academy, it seems imperative to consider the principally negative effect of specializations that have followed the contours of national aspirations and national languages, and of critical language that excludes all but fellow specialists. Medievalists, in particular, with so much material that echoes so richly with contemporary concerns, have a special opportunity to lead the way in returning our work to that sphere of public intellectual conversations of which it was once a part.

11. Giuseppe Mazzotta, *Dante Between Philosophers and Theologians: Paradiso X–XIII* (2000). Mazzotta raises one central, radical question: how Dante's understanding of poetry shapes his theology, his ethics, and, more generally his sense of the organization of knowledge or encyclopedias. By focusing on the cantos in the Heaven of the Sun, Giuseppe Mazzotta shows, first of all, the textual interrelationship holding together seemingly disparate thematic and conceptual patterns such as an extensive reflection on the Trinity, the issue of poverty among the Franciscans and Dominicans, and the dance of the wise spirits. What sustains the complexities of the text, Mazzotta argues, is Dante's insight into a *"theologia ludens,"* which embraces an ethics of risk as well as the notion of the joyful essence of the divinity.

12. Victoria Kirkham, *Dante the Book Glutton, Or, Food for Thought from Italian Poets* (2002). Boccaccio's *Little Treatise in Praise of Dante* (ca. 1350) documents his subject's love of learning with a story about how he went to Siena to see a book, then sat reading it all day with such absorption outside a shop on the piazza that he

failed to notice the noise from Palio festivities going on all around him. In the mid-fifteenth century, the humanist Manetti repeats this anecdote in his *Vita of Dante*, adding that like Cicero's Cato, the poet could be called "a book glutton" ("helluo libri"). The image of Dante as a book gobbler belongs to a rich Western tradition that runs from Ezechiel, St. John on Patmos, and Plato's *Symposium* via Augustine, Macrobius, Petrarch, and Dante himself, down into modern Italian fiction by Umberto Eco. The idea has visual counterparts in the typology of the author portrait, which depicts writers with their books from late antique models to medieval Gospels and secular Renaissance manuscripts. Most literary sources speak only of reading and "digesting" without pushing the metaphor to its logical conclusion. Martianus Capella (fifth cent.), however, imagines Lady Philology vomiting up books before her apotheosis as Mercury's bride. Commemorative statuary of a type known humorously in Italian as the "caccalibri" ("book pooper") completes the intellectual food cycle in another way, showing books streaming from behind Niccolò Tommaseo in Piazza Santo Stefano at Venice, and Benjamin Franklin on College Green at the University of Pennsylvania. John Crowe Ransom's amusing poem, "Survey of Literature," caps this illustrated history of literature as food for thought.

13. Rachel Jacoff, *Dante and the Jewish Question* (2003). Beginning with recent expressions of discomfort that two distinguished medievalists have noted in their relationship to texts that are at once beloved but also pernicious in their propagation of misogynistic and anti-Semitic clichés, this essay addresses Jacoff's own discomfort with Dante's reiteration of the deicide charge against the Jews in *Paradiso* 7 and elsewhere. It explores Dante's divergence from his major source, St. Anselm's *Cur deus homo,* and the implications of Anselm's own complex relationship to the Jews. The essay addresses the issue of the changing relationship of the medieval Church to the Jews in the thirteenth century and some of the theories that have been proposed by historians for the increasing sense of danger the Church manifests in this period. It concludes with a discussion of the issues at stake in teaching such issues and their pertinence to our own historical moment.

14. Christopher Kleinhenz, *Movement and Meaning in the Divine Comedy: Toward an Understanding of Dante's Processional Poetics From Divine to Human 39* (2005). Kleinhenz argues that an analysis of procession in the *Divine Comedy* is fundamental to an understanding of how Dante generates meaning in his poetic text. The entire *Comedy* may be seen as a procession during which Dante also observes an assortment of processions, which because of their formalized nature, have specific meaning for his journey. As Dante progresses toward his goal, he acquires knowledge, gains experience, and receives moral and spiritual enlightenment. His journey is at once linear and circular, linear in its progression toward the Beatific Vision and circular in that at the end of the poem he is once again returned to earth. The seeming conflict between linear and circular movement in the *Comedy* is resolved when Dante recognizes the linear process of transformation as the necessary preparatory stage for putting the soul in circular harmony with the celestial spheres.

15. William R. Cook and Ronald B. Herzman, *Dante From Two Perspectives: The Sienese Connection* (2007). Cook and Herzman combine the disciplines of history and literature to examine the Sienese whom Dante encounters in the *Purgatorio,* relating these characters and their stories to the interconnected histories of Florence and Siena in the generation preceding Dante's fictional journey in 1300, that is, to the generation of the battle of Montaperti (in 1260) and its aftermath. What Dante the pilgrim needs to learn, and what the lessons of the terraces of the proud and the envious teach him, especially in his encounter with Sienese such as Sapia and Provenzan Salvani, is the futility of seeing political activity in terms of winners and losers. This is the way that the Florentine Farinata degli Uberti—encountered by Dante the pilgrim in *Inferno* 10—looks at politics, and in that episode Dante the pilgrim seems perfectly willing to follow suit. In a somewhat systematic way, Dante the poet seems to be suggesting that the communal sin of Florence is Pride, and the communal sin of Siena is Envy. Cook and Herzman make the case that by the time Dante the pilgrim has finished his sojourn on the terrace of the envious, it can be seen that Siena is more likely to repent of its envy than Florence is of its pride. Therefore, the

treatment of Siena, and of the Sienese encountered in *Purgatory*, becomes an act of humility on the part of Dante the poet equivalent to that of Provenzan Salvani, who gained his salvation by begging in the Campo of Siena.

16. Dino S. Cervigni, *From Divine to Human: Dante's Circle vs. Boccaccio's Parodic Centers* (2009). From antiquity to our contemporary culture, the circle has always represented perfection. In the *Decameron,* Cevigni argues, Boccaccio employs circles and circularity from beginning to end; at the same time, he subverts the function of that millenary notion that attains its highest perfection in Dante. As a consequence of this new narrative strategy, Boccaccio, going beyond Dante and also Petrarch, seeks to create a new, less sacred but equally ethical, view of the world.

17. Albert Russell Ascoli, *'Favola fui': Petrarch Writes his Readers.* Building upon his 2008 book *Dante and the Making of a Modern Author*, Ascoli here reflects on the extent to which Petrarch's addresses to and figurations of his relationship to his readers intersect with the oft-asserted "modernity" of his authorial stances. In particular, Ascoli argues that following in the wake of Dante's double staging of himself as reader of his own works (especially in the *Vita Nuova*), Petrarch shows a keen and probing awareness of how the process of poetic signification involves a continual interchange between author and reader, as well as a strong desire to control the nature of that interchange as much as he can. Ascoli asserts that between Dante and Petrarch two primary—and contradictory—features of literary modernity can be identified: the affirmation of the preeminence of authorial intention and the foregrounding of readerly freedom of interpretation.

18. Lino Pertile, *Songs Beyond Mankind: Poetry and the Lager from Dante to Primo Levi* (2013). Is there is a degree of suffering and degradation beyond which a man or a woman ceases to be a human being? A point beyond which our soul dies and what survives is pure physiology? And if yes, to what extent may literature be capable of preserving our humanity in the face of unspeakable pain? These are some of the issues that this lecture explores by considering two systems of suffering, the hells described by Dante in his *Inferno* and Primo Levi in *Survival at Auschwitz*.

19. Zygmunt G. Barański, *Language as Sin and Salvation: A Lectura of* Inferno *18* (2014). With its sexual overtones and scatological references, *Inferno* 18 has caused considerable embarassment to Dante scholars, who have tended to offer partial and reductive readings of the canto. This essay aims to establish *Inferno* 18's key role in the structure of the *Commedia*, not only in its function as "prologue" to one of the most original sections of Dante's afterlife, the richly stratified circle of fraud Malebolge, but also as the canto in which the poet addresses two of the major controversial questions relating to the form of his great poem, namely, its status as "comedy" and its linguistic eclecticism.

20. Ronald L. Martinez, *Cleansing the Temple: Dante, Defender of the Church* (2017). Readers of the *Commedia* are familiar with Dante's severe judgment of contemporary popes. The attacks are explicable as part of Dante's strategy of defending the Church itself, which the poet saw as imperiled by papal avarice and political ambition. From the reference to the biblical punishment of Uzzah for touching the Ark of the Covenant in *Epistola* XI, urging Italian cardinals at the 1314 conclave to elect a Pope favorable to Rome, we know that Dante anticipated accusations of meddling in Church affairs. And meddle he did: the representations in the poem of the Church, in guises both historical and typological (Ark of the Covenant, Temple, Bride of Christ, etc.) comprise an ambitious program by which Dante identifies with the role of protector and purifier of the Church, modeled chiefly on scriptural episodes of Christ cleansing the Temple, long used within the Church itself in order to spur anti-simoniacal reform. A series of passages in the second half of *Paradiso* (Cantos 15–16, 18, 22, 27) elaborate Dante's investment in this role, one that is repeatedly linked to the poet's condition as an exile.

STATE UNIVERSITY OF NEW YORK PRESS
www.sunypress.edu

ISBN: 978-1-4384-8694-9